IMAGES
of Scotland

LANARK AND THE CLYDE VALLEY

To Anne and Robert
Best Wishes
Helen Moir

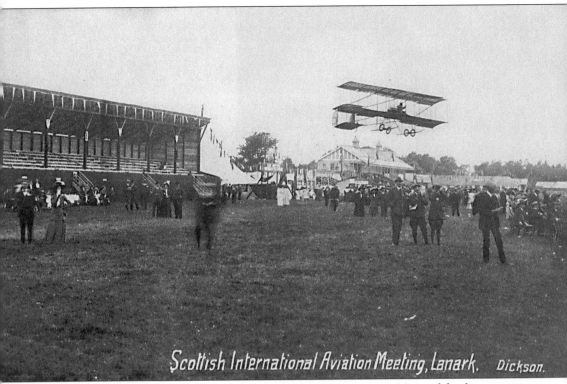

Scottish International Aviation Meeting, Lanark. Dickson.

The first aviation meeting in Scotland took place at the racecourse Many of the famous aviators of the time took part and they brought a selection of different aircraft to wow the crowds with. Over 100,000 people attended and there were special trains to the event. There was even a special postmark used on many of the postcards sent from the meeting. These photographs were probably taken on the first day and were for sale well before the event finished.

Lanark, Race Course, Aviation Ground

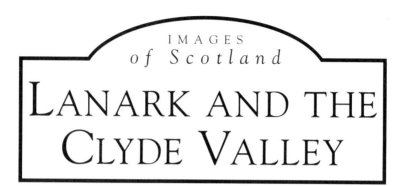

IMAGES
of Scotland

LANARK AND THE CLYDE VALLEY

Compiled by
Helen Moir

TEMPUS

Tempus Publishing Limited
The Mill, Brimscombe Port,
Stroud, Gloucestershire, GL5 2QG

ISBN 0 7524 1757 6

Typesetting and origination by
Tempus Publishing Limited
Printed in Great Britain by
Midway Clark Printing, Wiltshire

New Lanark in the mid-1960s. At this time some of the mills were totally derelict and with their roofs off. It is the dedication and hard work of many people that has made the village the World Heritage Site that it is today.

Contents

Acknowledgements

I would like to give a very special thank to the following people and institutions:
Hamilton Advertiser; Lanark Grammar School; John McKillop; Lanark Loch Hotel; M. Howatson; Lanark Police Station; Lanark Golf Club; David Brown; Margaret Perrie; Mr and Mrs Raeside; Ron Harris; George Topp; *Carluke and Lanark Advertiser*; *Lanark Gazette*; Lanark Library; Paul Archibald; New Lanark Conservation and Civic Trust; Lorna Davidson; Richard Evans; Jim Arnold; The Original Tearoom; Agnes and Frank Yates; Douglas T. Miller; Rosebank Productions; Gilmour Crossford; Douglas McMillan; Martin Boyd; The Gordon Public House; Clyde Valley Tourist Board; Jim Cleary; Kim, Manageress at Lanark Loch Hotel; Constable Kenny Ellis; John Letham; Lanark Tourist Information Office.

A special mention is due to John McKillop Lanarkshire Legacy Series and the *Hamilton Advertidser* photographers for their kind donation of material for this book.

I also wish to thank my husband Bill Moir for his marvellous support and encouragement.

This book could not have been accomplished without the help and donations from all these people and institution.

Introduction

The ancient market town of Lanark sits perched on high sloping ground above the valley of the Clyde. The town sits about five to six hundred feet above sea level. Below it runs the Clyde, which flows through a series of gorges in the vicinity of Lanark before winding its way past Hamilton and onwards to Glasgow and the sea. The area is known as Upper Clydesdale and forms part of the administrative region of South Lanarkshire. Lanark is in the rural part of the county and heavy industry has managed to pass the town by. The immediate area is composed of rolling hills and productive farmland. The town and its surrounding villages have been the market garden for Glasgow for over two hundred years, and market gardening and garden centres are still very much an integral part of the local rural economy.

The origins of the name of Lanark are supposedly of Cumbrian origin and the word 'lanerc' means a glade or clear spot. There has been a settlement here for many centuries and the accepted date of the town being created a Royal Burgh is 1140. There would have been a settlement here for many years beforehand. Royal Burgh status conferred on the town the right to hold a market and to levy taxes on imports into the town.

The area abounds with ancient settlements, suggesting inhabitation from over 4,000 years ago. It was an important religous centre and the earliest church in the town is St Nicholas, for which a reference is made around 1214. The current St Nicholas church was erected in 1774 and has a statue of Scotland's greatest hero, William Wallace.

The old church of St Kentigern's on Hyndford Road dates from the fifteenth century and was once known as the Out Kirk, being outwith the burgh. The early religous history of the area dates back almost to the Roman period, when men like St Kentigern (also known as St Mungo), St Ninian, St Serf, St Nethan and St Machan were active in the local area. References to these holy men are found in local place names all round the county.

Famous names associated with the town include William Wallace, who lived with his wife, Marion Braidfute, in a house in the Castlegate. The legend goes that Wallace killed a few English soldiers and hid in a cave near where the Cartland bridge crosses a deep ravine. The Sheriff of Lanark, Sir William Heselrig, had Wallace's house burned and his wife killed. Wallace sought revenge, killed the sheriff and burned the garrison. Wallace, with his small but growing band, took on the might of the English and defeated them at Stirling in 1296. He was captured at Falkirk and hung, drawn and quartered.

Robert the Bruce and a few other Scottish kings, including Alexander II and William the First, stayed at Lanark Castle. There are no remains left of Lanark Castle, which was situated on the Castlegate.

Robert the Bruce granted land in the Bloomgate for a friary. This was on land where the Clydesdale Hotel now stands.

Lanark has produced other famous people including William Lithgow, the famous traveller; William Smellie, the obstetrician; William Roy, of Ordnance Survey map fame and John Glaister, a renowned forensic scientist. The quality of education in the town was the making of these people – established over 800 years ago, is the oldest school in Scotland.

An ancient tradition in the town has been Lanimer Day. The Lanimer event is held in June and is based on the tradition of walking the boundary of the town. On the final day there is a procession in the town as well as the crowning of the Lanimer Queen under the statue of William Wallace at St Nicholas church.

Lanark was also made famous in the early part of the nineteenth century with the establishment of the Utopian-style mills at New Lanark. The mills were built in one of the gorges and used the unlimited energy of the Clyde to provide power to operate the machinery. The mills produced cloth and the owner, Robert Owen, worked on the principle that better fed, better educated employees produced better quality work in less time. While conditions at New Lanark were still harsh, they were infinitely better than those in other mills where the workers were exploited.

Founded by David Dale, and passed to his son-in-law, Owen, the mills at New Lanark are now a World Heritage Site, recognized throughout the world as one of the first workplaces where the workers were cared for and their lives bettered by their employers.

Lanark is still a thriving market town with much to recommend it to visitors and locals alike. It has a good range of shops, has a place in many different periods of Scottish history and has played a major part in the growth of our nation. Residents of the town have made an impact throughout the world and the modern-day lanarkians are hard-working, friendly folk who have every right to be proud of their town and its long, colourful history.

One
Lanark

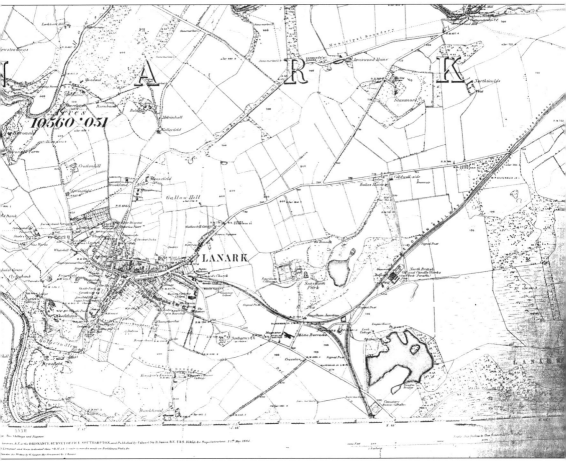

Lanark, 1864, from a map held in Lanark library.

Lanark High Street looking down to the foot of the town. St Nicholas church is the oldest still in use in Lanark and a statue of Sir William Wallace looks down from the church. *Courtesy of Hamilton Advertiser.*

A *c*.1930s view of the High Street. Prior to 1730 the High Street was known as the 'Hietoun'. The building on the left-hand side at the bottom of the street was the Tolbooth. *Courtsy of Lanark Grammar.*

Bannatyne Street with the Caledeonian Hotel, which was demolished in 1998. After the railway line was constructed to Lanark, many hotels were built around the new station and Lanark became a desirable place to go on holiday, having clean air and being at a reasonable altitude. *Courtesy of John McKillop, Lanarkshire Legacy Series.*

Greenside Lane looking from Hope Street. *Courtesy of Hamilton Advertiser.*

A modern view of Castlegate. *Courtesy of the Hamilton Advertiser.*

Wellgatehead with, on the corner, the Corra Linn public house. This pub is named after one of the falls on the Clyde. *Courtesy of John McKillop, Lanarkshire Legacy Series.*

The top of High Street where it becomes St Leonard's Street. It was the site of the Lanark Co-op which has long ago vacated the site. *Courtesy of John McKillop, Lanarkshire Legacy Series.*

The top of the old Co-op building in Lanark. Note the handshake 'Unitas' which is a symbol of the co-operative movement. Robert Owen played a large part in the foundation of co-operatives with his radical ideas at New Lanark. *Courtesy of John McKillop, Lanarkshire Legacy Series.*

The ruins of the old St Kentigern's church in Hyndford Road. It was known as the 'Out Kirk' because it stood just outwith the burgh boundaries. This is the church where William Wallace was reputed to have met Marion Braidfute. *Courtesy of Hamilton Advertiser.*

An old gravestone in St Kentigern's graveyard. It is the last resting-place for James Barr, a local shoemaker, who died in 1767 aged only twenty-seven. *Courtesy of John McKillop, Lanarkshire Legacy Series.*

An angel guards another person's resting place in St Kentigern's. *Courtesy of John McKillop, Lanarkshire Legacy Series.*

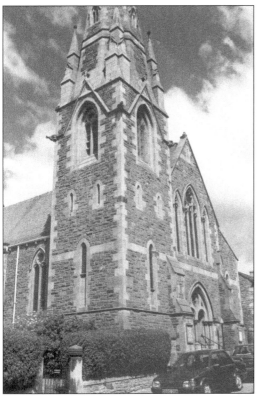

The new St Kentigern's church in Hope Street. The building was constructed in the nineteenth century. *Courtesy of Hamilton Advertiser.*

A close-up view of the statue of William Wallace at St Nicholas church. The sculptor was Robert Forrest and his inspiration was an old illustration in the possession of the Society of Antiquaries. *Courtesy of Hamilton Advertiser.*

Castlebank House was built in or just prior to 1780 for Mr John Bannatyne. The house was divided into flats in the 1950s and totally refurbished in 1996. Bannatyne Street was named after John Bannatyne. *Courtesy of Hamilton Advertiser.*

The William Smellie Maternity Hospital is sadly no longer in use. Smellie was a renowned leading light in obstetrics. *Courtesy of Hamilton Advertiser.*

'Motherhood', a statue which once stood outside the William Smellie Maternity Hospital. It was presented to the town by Emeritus Professor Samuel J. Cameron, of the Chair of Midwifery in the University of Glasgow, in memory of Smellie. After closure of the hospital the statue was removed and placed in the entrance foyer of the health centre in the South Vennel. *Courtesy of Hamilton Advertiser.*

Smyllum House was owned by William Smellie, who had it built around 1759 and lived there till he died in 1763. He is buried in a chapel attached to the old ruined church of St Kentigern's. Every year a wreath is still placed on his grave. The house was originally called Smellum, then Smillum and finally Smyllum. In 1792, the property was purchased by William Honeyman, son-in-law of Lord Braxfield. He altered the house greatly. Its next owner was the Roman Catholic Church, who turned it in to an orphanage, for which purpose it was used from 1864 to 1980. Mr Robert Monteith of Carstairs helped fund the purchase of the house. The house is reputed to be haunted by a bowler-hatted gentleman. He has been seen walking down the driveway by motorists, but they lose sight of him around a bend in the road. The house now stands derelict. *Courtesy of Hamilton Advertiser.*

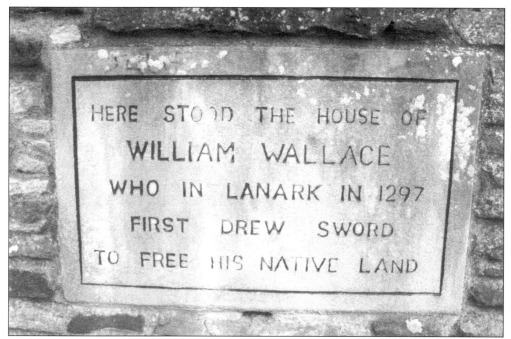

This plaque is attached to the monument that stands in the Castlegate. *Courtesy of John McKillop, Lanarkshire Legacy Series.*

The High Street looking upwards. *Courtesy of Hamilton Advertiser.*

A view of the foot of the High Street. *Courtesy of Hamilton Advertiser.*

Station Square c.1910. *Courtesy of Lanark Loch Hotel.*

Lanark Loch was man-made and was formerly marshland. It was turned into a loch and was used at one point to help supply the town with water. The loch was extended in the 1840s, at which time it was known as Marr's Loch. Hugh Marr was an architect who devised a scheme to supply the town with water from the loch. There were problems with the pumping machinery and with the water levels and the scheme was abandoned in 1870.

Lanark Loch is a popular spot for both tourists and locals. During the early part of the twentieth century it and the surrounding area were used for training soldiers when they had camps in the locality.

The refurbished Lanark Loch Hotel is now owned by Brewers Fayre. *Courtesy of Bill Moir.*

Lanark Loch, 2000. *Courtesy of Bill Moir.*

Lanark Loch is a peaceful place and is well used on summer weekends and evenings.

The arched entrance to the Lady Hozier Convalescent Home in Hyndford Road. *Courtesy of John McKillop, Lanarkshire Legacy Series.*

Lady Hozier Convalescent Home, Lanark

Sir William Hozier of Maudslie offered to provide Glasgow Royal Infirmary with the above home which was to be named after his wife. The site of the former Lanark Militia Barracks (which had been demolished in 1880) was purchased and the Lady Hozier Convalescent Home was opened in 1893. It had a capacity of forty-two patients. *Courtesy of the Lanark Loch Hotel.*

The Lady Hozier Memorial Home is now run by the of Lanarkshire Health Board. *Courtesy of Hamilton Advertiser.*

Bellefield Sanatorium. *Courtsy of M. Howatson, Motherwell.*

Lanark railway station. The railway came to Lanark in the 1850s and was on a branch from the main line to Glasgow and Edinburgh. A terminal was built here and the lovely station building still stands today. *Courtesy of Bill Moir.*

A Glasgow-bound train ready to leave. The station is much frequented by commuters to Glasgow who have chosen to live in the midst of the Clyde Valley. *Courtesy of Bill Moir.*

Lanark's busy Tourist Information centre. With all its attractions and beautiful scenery, Lanark is well served to cater for tourists, whether daytrippers or those who come for longer. *Courtesy of Bill Moir.*

Hyndford Bridge, near Lanark, built in 1773. My grandfather was called David Hynd and was descended from Lanark domestic weavers.

Two
Men in Uniform

Constable Kenny Ellis at the launch of Farm Week in February 1998. The bull is named Magician. *Courtesy of Lanark Police Station*.

Present here at the same event at Lanark Market are local farmers, the managing director of Lawrie Symington, as well as Chief Inspector David Chadwick, Constable Kenny Ellis, Councillor Irene Logan, market staff and, of course, Magician. *Courtesy of Lanark Police Station.*

Stanmore House, May 1997, with the local police performing some of their community duties. *Courtesy of Lanark Police Station.*

28

Right and below: Photographs taken during Community Safety Week in July 1999. Penguin Pete is Andy Nixon of Lanark Police Station, while the elephant is one of the local firemen. *Courtesy of Lanark Police Station.*

'Safe as Houses' is a joint venture between South Lanarkshire Council and the police Crime Prevention Unit. A package was supplied to many households giving advice on all aspects of home security. Shown here is a presentation of a 'Safe as Houses' pack. *Courtesy of Lanark Police Station.*

Pub Safety Week in 1998. A view taken in Lanark High Street. The officers are Constable Kenny Ellis and Sergeant Mary Wilson. *Courtesy of Lanark Police Station.*

Three

Schools

The Sixth Form at Lanark Grammar school in 1970. The school is over 800 years old and is the oldest in Scotland. *Courtesy of Lanark Grammar*.

The class of '57. Class 2B in 1957 at Lanark Grammar.

You will surely remember some of these teachers. The staff at Lanark Grammar in 1965.

The senior football team at Lanark Grammar in the 1955/56 season. *Courtesy of Lanark Grammar*.

This is the Lanark Grammar football club reserve team of 1956/57. The team was often successful and won many games. *Courtesy of Lanark Grammar*.

Lanark Grammar and some surrounding landmarks seen from the air.

Another view of the grammar school as viewed from the air.

Four
Recreation

GOLF COURSE & CLUB HOUSE, SHEWING TINTO IN DISTANCE, LANARK.   A.3076.

Visible in the background of this view of Lanark Golf Club is the hill, Tinto.

Lanark Golf Club is thought to be the seventeenth oldest in Britain and was laid out in 1851, the year of the Great Exhibition at Crystal Palace, London. *Courtesy of Hamilton Advertiser.*

A view towards Lanark Loch and Tinto from the Golf Club.

When the course was first laid out in 1851 it had only six holes. It rose to eighteen by 1897 as a result of extensions over the years. Now a nine-hole course runs alongside the eighteen-hole one.

Curling is one of those sports which can only be played in the right conditions, which, with global warming, are becoming rarer outdoors nowadays. This view is of curling at the Golf Club.

Lanark Racecourse ceased to be used as such in the 1970s. Its major trophy was the famous Silver Bell. Legends of the bell go back to William the Lion, who supposedly introduced racing to Lanark in 1160. The Silver Bell itself was probably made in Edinburgh sometime around 1610. *Courtesy of Hamilton Advertiser*.

Lanark racecourse and the Tote. It isn't widely known but the Tote is a government-owned betting shop chain. It must rate as one of our more unusual nationalized industries.

Five

Do you Recognize Anyone?

The Wallace March is held annually in August by members of the Wallace Society. They are seen here walking down the High Street towards St Nicholas church where a wreath is traditionally laid under the statue of the great man himself and a memorial service is held. The two men at the front are carrying a replica of Wallace's huge broadsword. Wallace himself was captured by the English and hung, drawn and quartered in London in 1305.

A gathering for a local function taken outside St Nicholas church in the 1940s.

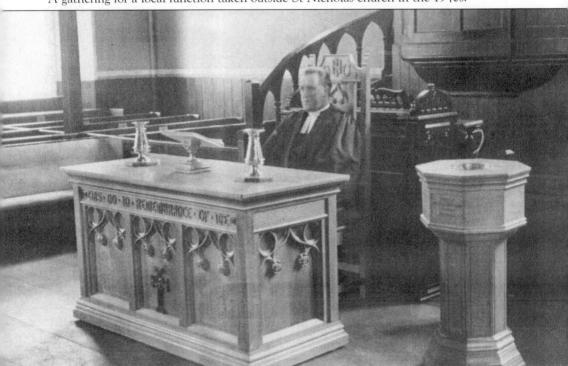
The Revd Mr Limmond of St Leonard's church.

This gentleman was called Mr Wright and he worked at Lumsden's lemonade factory.

The Lanark area caters for many thousands of tourists per year. Many gravitate towards Lanark Tourist Information Centre (TIC) and here are some of the staff of the Tourist Board, photographed beside the Clyde.

The seat shown here used to be outside St Nicholas church. Here the minister, the Revd Marcus Dickson, has a blether with some locals.

Two of the staff of Lanark TIC inside their office. *Courtesy of Bill Moir*.

The staff of Carfin House. The house belonged to the Graham family. The gentleman sitting at the end of the front row with the dog is Mr David Brown, great grandfather of David Brown the shoemaker. *Courtesy of Mr David Brown.*

Mr J. Calderwood outside the co-op in New Lanark. *Courtesy of Margaret Perrie.*

The 1958 Lanimer Day. Queen Sandra Nelson and members of her court are distributing Lanimer medals to the procession entrants at Lanark Higher Grade School. Also in the photograph are Margaret Perrie and Christine McFarlane. *Courtesy of Margaret Perrie.*

Queen Margaret and her court at the Rechabite Gala, Crossford, 1938. *Courtesy of Margaret Perrie.*

Six
Business

The blacksmith's in the Bloomgate. It is now the site of a tearoom called 'Daisies'. *Courtesy of Mr and Mrs Raeside.*

Daisies Tearoom is run by Mr and Mrs Raeside.

The inside of the tearoom. What a contrast from when it was a blacksmith's.

Here is the Lanimer Room inside Daisies. Around the walls are numerous scenes of bygone Lanimer days.

Ristorante La Vigna in the Wellgate. *Courtesy Hamilton Advertiser.*

The Clydesdale Hotel was built in 1791 but is sadly no more. The building was on the site of a friary which was in ruins by 1566. *Courtesy of Hamilton Advertiser.*

Lanark Auction Market is still very successful and was set up around 1840 by Mr John Lawrie. By 1862 he had taken his nephew, James Symington, into partnership with him. The market was originally at the bottom of Hope Street and moved to its present site in 1867. The business was acquired by William Hope early in the last century. *Courtesy of Hamilton Advertiser.*

A modern industrial estate, looking towards Cleghorn. *Courtesy of Hamilton Advertiser.*

The skinworks in the North Vennel.

Demolition of the old skinworks in the North Vennel.

The Royal Oak Hotel in Woodstock Road.

David Brown's shoemakers in Wellgatehead. This view, of around 1912, is of the shopfront. In the photograph, from left to right, are: T. Cairns, J. O'Leary, David Brown, Jessie McHardy, J. Hamilton and A. Henderson. *Courtesy of Mr David Brown.*

David Brown's first shop in Bloomgate. The man in the white apron is old David Brown himself. His grandson still operates a family business in the town today. *Courtesy of Mr David Brown.*

The interior of the Bloomgate shop. *Courtesy of Mr David Brown.*

J. Wilson's bootmakers in Wellgate with David Brown standing at the far right. *Courtesy of Mr David Brown.*

David Brown's shop in the High Street, *c*.1934.

The Birks was established in 1834 and is now called the Gordon. It is in Ladyacre Road.

Looking up from St Nicholas church to the top of the High Street.

Looking down from the top of the High Street. It is always amazing to look at views like this and see the different shops and businesses.

Seven

The Lanimers

Leigh Mulligan, Lanimer Queen of 1986, being crowned. *Courtesy of Hamilton Advertiser.*

Wilma Keay, Lanimer
Queen of 1983. *Courtesy
of Hamilton Advertiser*.

Annie, Lanimer Queen of 1939, the year the
war broke out.

Elaine McLintock about to be crowned in 1978. *Courtesy of Hamilton Advertiser*.

Senga Hamilton being crowned in 1968 by Mrs William Toy. *Courtesy of Hamilton Advertiser*.

Lynn Green being crowned by Mrs Moira Stoddart. *Courtesy of Hamilton Advertiser*.

Gaye Galloway was the Lanimer Queen in 1979. *Courtesy of Hamilton Advertiser*.

The Lanimer Queen and her court of 1995. *Courtesy of Hamilton Advertiser.*

The Lanimer Queen and her court of 1998. *Courtesy of Hamilton Advertiser.*

The Lanimer Queen being crowned in 1971. *Courtesy of Hamilton Advertiser*.

The 1984 Lanimer Queen being crowned. *Courtesy of Hamilton Advertiser.*

The crowning of the 1992 Lanimer Queen. *Courtesy of Hamilton Advertiser.*

61

The 1993 Lanimer Queen is crowned. *Courtesy of Hamilton Advertiser.*

The 1996 Lanimer Queen is crowned. *Courtesy of Hamilton Advertiser.*

The Lanimer Queen of 1981 is crowned.
Courtesy of Hamilton Advertiser.

The Lanimer Queen and her court of c.1913.

The Lanimer Queen of 1977 arrives at the Lanimer Ball on the arm of the Lord Cornet, Mr John Barrie. *Courtesy of Hamilton Advertiser.*

Tracey Wallace, Queen of 1977, with Lord Cornet Dr Bill Criggie, outside the Cartland Bridge Hotel. *Courtesy of Hamilton Advertiser.*

Some of the Lord Cornets during the 1980 Lanimer celebrations. The Lanimer event lasts for a week, beginning on the Sunday with the 'kirkin' of the Lord Cornet, or Standard Bearer, in St Nicholas Church. On Monday is the perambulation of the marches, where the boundaries of the town are walked round. On Tuesday evening a ball is held and on Wednesday, the Lord Cornet leads a cavalcade to inspect the remainder of the boundaries. On Thursday, Lanimer Day, the grand procession takes place with a multitude of decorated floats and the crowning of the Lanimer Queen under the statue of Wallace. *Courtesy of Hamilton Advertiser*.

Lord Cornets at the Boundary Stone enjoying a toast. *Courtesy Hamilton Advertiser*.

Lanimer celebrations c.1971. A lot of hard work and planning goes into this important event. The children are carrying a banner relating to Lockhart and the Lee Penny. The Lockhart family owned Lee Castle and the story of the Lee Penny comes from the period of the Crusades. A member of the Lockhart family took hostage a Moorish prince or nobleman, whose family paid a ransom of a heart-shaped jewel. This was set into a silver fourpenny, or groat, and supposedly had magic healing powers. The penny is still in the family. *Courtesy of Hamilton Advertiser*.

A Clydesdale horse gaily decorated during the Lanimer celebrations of c.1936.

Eight
New Lanark

Robert Owen's house is on the left of this photograph of New Lanark. He married David Dale's daughter Caroline in 1799 and helped run the mills at New Lanark with two other partners. Owen held deep socialist views and the ideas he put into practice at New Lanark were far ahead of any of the time. He realised that better conditions at both work and home would increase productivity. *Courtesy of Hamilton Advertiser*.

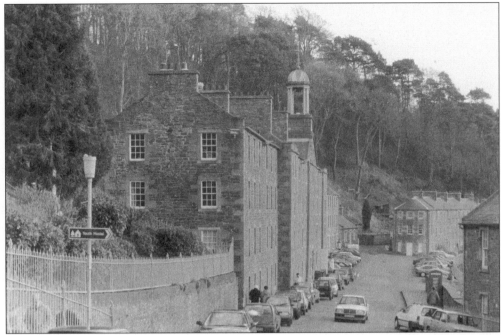

The entrance to New Lanark in 1995. For many years a derelict industrial site, the mills were acquired by the New Lanark Conservation & Civic Trust in 1974. Many of the houses have been re-inhabited and the mills restored to form a huge museum. Well worth a visit today, the mills are now a World Heritage Site. *Courtesy of Hamilton Advertiser.*

New Lanark looking towards Dundaff Linn. The mills were built here because of the unlimited source of water power running down the valley of the Clyde. The mills themselves were used to manufacture cloth and once housed huge, noisy, belt-driven looms. *Courtesy of Hamilton Advertiser.*

Long Row, New Lanark. These houses have been modernized and are all inhabited. Conditions apply to purchasers and they are not allowed to have satellite dishes or other fixtures on the outside of their houses. *Courtesy of Hamilton Advertiser.*

Mill workers c.1890. They are sitting on the school steps. *Courtesy of New Lanark Conservation & Civic Trust.*

Jessie Stewart was born in 1854 and here she is standing outside her house in Caithness Row, c.1905. *Courtesy of New Lanark Conservation & Civic Trust.*

Villagers at New Lanark *c.*1890. *Courtesy of New Lanark Conservation & Civic Trust.*

A view of New Lanark during the Second World War. Throughout the war the workers made camouflage netting. *Courtesy of New Lanark Conservation & Civic Trust.*

71

As well as camouflage netting, tarpaulins were also manufactured at New Lanark. Here are some of the workers during the war. *Courtesy of New Lanark Conservation & Civic Trust.*

New Lanark in 1974 when Jim Callaghan visited. He is seen here with Jim Arnold, director of New Lanark Conservation & Civic Trust. Also in the picture is Dame Judith Hart, the local MP at the time. Jim Arnold is still with the Trust. *Courtesy of Hamilton Advertiser.*

Much has happened at New Lanark in the last twenty-five years. There has been a lot of restoration work and those who visited in 1974 would be hard pushed to recognize the scenes there today, as the village has been revitalized and the buildings restored. Here are Jim Arnold (left) and Harry Smith, two of the leading lights in the Trust and Board of Trustees. *Courtesy of Hamilton Advertiser*.

A view of the inside of the village store at New Lanark. *Courtesy of Hamilton Advertiser*.

Jim Cuthbertson, of Carstairs, operating nineteenth-century spinning mules. Visitors to the mills can see this machinery operating. When the mill was fully functioning there would be many of these machines in here and the noise would have been unbelievable. *Courtesy of Hamilton Advertiser*.

Arthur Bell, owner of Scotland Direct, and his wife, Susan, outside the Counting House in the 1970s. *Courtesy of Hamilton Advertiser*.

From left to right: Mr Arthur Bell, Mr Jim Arnold, Director of the New Lanark Conservation and Civic Trust, and trustees Walter Nisbit and Cedric Wilson. *Courtesy Hamilton Advertiser.*

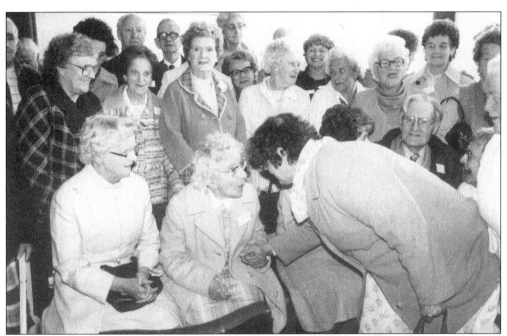

Ida Smith, aged ninety-two, meeting some of her former pupils at the New Lanark Village reunion. Miss Smith was a well-loved and respected teacher at New Lanark School. She later taught at Lanark Grammar. The lady speaking to her is Margaret Nicol, wife of John, mill manager from 1911 to 1946. The photo dates from August 1985. *Courtesy of New Lanark Conservation & Civic Trust.*

A lovely view of New Lanark.

New Lanark is in a picturesque setting set into the valley of the Clyde as it passes through a gorge. It is the unique setting which led to the mills being established here.

The New Buildings, which have now been restored. The bell at the top of the building is the Caithness Bell, which was once rung to call workers to the factory and also to announce Sunday service. *Courtesy of Hamilton Advertiser.*

New Lanark, *c.*1996. *Courtesy of Hamilton Advertiser.*

Refurbishment work at New Lanark in 1997. Much has been done in twenty-five years and the site is a tribute to those who have made it possible. *Courtesy of Hamilton Advertiser.*

Robert Owen, manager and owner of New Lanark from 1788-1825. He was a forward-thinking man and his schemes and ideas were far ahead of his time. Workers could take any grievance direct to Owen if they deemed that they had been unfairly treated. *Courtesy of New Lanark Conservation & Civic Trust.*

Nine

The Clyde Valley and the Orchard Country

The Garrion Bridge was built in the eighteenth century and remains the same today except for the toll house, which was demolished a long time ago. Plans are afoot to build another bridge about fifty yards down river to alleviate the traffic congestion here today.

This is the inscription on a stone panel on the Garrion Bridge. At the time the bridge was built there was no safe crossing of the Clyde from Lanark to Bothwell.

Dalserf Church sits in the village of Dalserf, which was once the principal town in Dalserf Parish. The church was built in 1655 and is still thriving. Nowadays the congregation is led by Revd Cameron McPherson.

Dalserf Church has two open days a
year in May and September and is well
worth attending. The church is
referred to as the 'Auld Grey Mother
Kirk', a name given to it by the Revd
William Peebles Rorison, who served
as a minister from 1851-1907.

The old manse in Dalserf village. The manse was built at the same time as the church and has
now been replaced as the manse by a new one a short distance away.

At one time a ferry crossed the Clyde here at Dalserf.

Dalserf village in a photograph by John McKillop. *Courtesy of Lanarkshire Legacy Series.*

Dalserf village and church. *Courtesy of John McKillop, Lanarkshire Legacy Series*.

The gatehouse to the now-demolished Maudslie Castle. The bridge spans the Clyde and once led to Maudslie. *Courtesy of Bill Moir*.

MAULDSLIE CASTLE, CARLUKE.

Maudslie Castle was built in 1793 by Thomas Carmichael, 5th Earl of Hyndford. It was purchased in 1850 by James Hozier, of Newlands and Barrowfield. Winston Churchill married Clementina Hozier in 1908. *Courtesy of Douglas T. Miller, Rosebank Productions.*

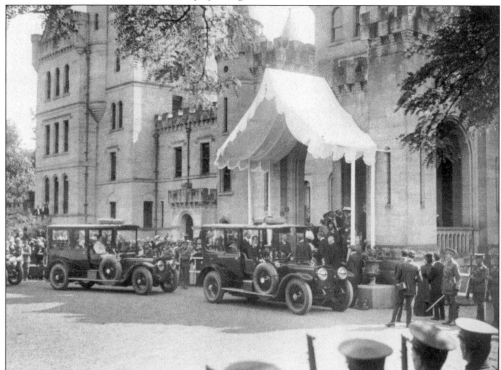

George V and Queen Mary arrive at Maudslie Castle as guests of the Newland's family in 1914. *Courtesy of Douglas T. Miller, Rosebank Productions.*

The crest of James Hozier, Lord
Newlands. *Courtesy of Douglas T. Miller,
Rosebank Productions.*

Rosebank village and the Popinjay Hotel in the 1930s. Many of the families in Rosebank
worked for Lord Newlands and the Maudslie estate. Lord Newlands had the village refurbished.
Courtesy of Douglas T. Miller, Rosebank Productions.

The Popinjay Hotel today. The hotel is very popular. *Courtesy of Bill Moir*.

A *c.*1900 view of the Rosebank Inn. The inn was replaced by the very Tudor-looking Popinjay Hotel not long after this photograph was taken. The name 'Popinjay' comes from a multi-coloured parrot-like effigy used for archery practice. There is a mention in Walter Scott's *Old Mortality*. *Courtesy of Douglas T. Miller, Rosebank Productions*.

Rosebank village today. The road is now part of the Clyde Valley Tourist Route and is well-used by both locals and day trippers from Glasgow and other parts of Lanarkshire. A number of garden centres and tourist attractions have sprung up in the villages along the route. *Courtesy of Bill Moir.*

The Rosebank Coffee Shop is a typical example of the many and varied attractions in the area. *Courtesy of Bill Moir.*

The entrance to what was once Milton Lockhart Castle. Milton Lockhart was built for William Lockhart in 1829. William was a half brother of John Gibson Lockhart, son-in-law of Sir Walter Scott and it was Scott, who chose the site. The house began to fall into decline in the 1920s and deteriorated badly over the years. It was purchased in 1987 by a Japanese businessman who had it shipped stone by stone to Japan, where it was re-assembled in a theme park. *Courtesy of Bill Moir.*

The gatehouse to Milton Lockhart.

This is the once-proud house at Milton Lockhart that now resides in Hokkaido. *Courtesy of Douglas T. Miller, Rosebank Productions.*

Milton Lockhart just prior to dismantling. *Courtesy of Douglas T. Miller, Rosebank Productions.*

The estate housed many workers and the farm is seen here.

Lee Castle was built between 1834 and 1845 for Sir Norman Lockhart. The Barony of Lee was granted to William Loccard in 1272. His son, Symon, was knighted by Robert the Bruce. He left Scotland with the Black Douglas to take Bruce's heart to the Holy Land, but their journey was interrupted at Seville where they fought the Moors. Bruce's heart never made it to the Holy Land and was instead buried at Dryburgh Abbey. *Courtesy of the Hamilton Advertiser.*

90

The Lee Penny, once located in the Castle, is one of the most famous artefacts in the area and was brought back from Spain by Symon Loccard as ransom for the life of a Moorish nobleman. The red heart-shaped stone was set into a penny in the time of Edward IV of England. *Courtesy of Douglas T. Miller, Rosebank Productions.*

Craignethan Castle is another local site linked to Sir Walter Scott. Also known as Tillietudlem, it was the inspiration for Scott's *Old Mortality*. The castle was a stronghold of the Hamilton family and was built around 1532 by Sir James Hamilton of Finnart. He was the illegitimate son of James Hamilton, 1st Earl of Arran. *Courtesy of Douglas T. Miller, Rosebank Productions.*

Craignethan in more recent times. The castle has been a tourist attraction for a long time and views of it have been sold since before the advent of the picture postcard. The old Caledonian Railway issued a set of the local area to sell to day trippers.

The Clyde Valley Tourist Route takes one past many garden centres all the way from the Garrion Bridge to Lanark itself. These have grown out of the nurseries and market gardens that were the mainstay of local agriculture and kept the industrial belt supplied with fresh fruit and vegetables. This is the Snadyholm Garden Centre. *Courtesy of Bill Moir.*

Crossford in a more tranquil time. *Courtesy of Douglas T. Miller, Rosebank Productions.*

Crossford village.

The School house in Crossford.

Lanark Road, Crossford, as it once was when it was still called Main Street.

Crossford village today showing the contrast in this small settlement.

White water rafting past Crossford village on the Clyde.

More views of rafting in 1994.

White water rafting, Crossford, 1994.

Some of the rafting is done for charity. Here some musicians get ready to sail off on their double bass.

The toll-house for the bridge that crosses the Clyde at Crossford. In the eighteenth century, in an attempt to improve the road network, private individuals and companies built decent roads and charged a toll to use them. There are many of these toll-houses scattered around the country at strategic points where travellers had no option but to pay.

If the toll-houses were not at points like river crossings or junctions unscrupulous travellers could bypass them and avoid the tolls. Tolls would vary depending on the mode of transport and on the size of the vehicle.

The Tillietudlem Hotel now stands derelict but it was once owned by George Young the famous footballer. A 1920s bullnose Morris sits at the front of the hotel.

The Post Office at Crossford sometime in the 1920s The delivery van parked in front of it is probably an Austin or a Ford.

A tranquil view of the village of Crossford.

Crossford war memorial is built next to a spring called 'Sannys'.

The Carfin estate at Crossford is now a country park. Here is a small railway with a locomotive named after General Roy. *Courtesy of John McKillop, Lanarkshire Legacy Series.*

Ross and Lewis McKillop at the Clyde Valley Country Estate. *Courtesy of John McKillop, Lanarkshire Legacy Series.*

Carfin House was built in the early nineteenth century and went through a series of owners before being demolished. In 1824 a family called Nisbit lived there. By 1870 the Steel family owned the house and renamed it Holmhead House. In 1880 James Noble bought the house and renamed it Carfin. His family was in the wine and port business and vast sums were spent improving the house and estate. Many locals were employed there. Carfin House sadly met the fate of many large houses in the 1930s and was demolished.

This suspension bridge leads from the Clyde Valley Road to the Clyde Valley Estate.

Hazelbank village.

A 1996 photograph of disabled athletes. The duck race replaced white water rafting in the mid-1990s.

A view of the duck race at Hazelbank.

Stonebyres House was demolished in 1934. James Noble Graham of Carfin purchased the house from Miss Monteith-Scott in 1906. It was bought back by Miss Monteith-Scott in 1924 and was demolished after her death in 1934. *Courtesy of Douglas T. Miller, Rosebank Productions.*

The hydro-electric power station at Stonebyres was built in 1927 and generates six megawatts. *Courtesy of Bill Moir*

Kirkfieldbank looking from the steep Lanark Brae. At the top of the brae is a capstan used for pulling traction engines up the hill in the olden days. *Courtesy of Douglas T. Miller, Rosebank Productions.*

Main Street, Kirkfieldbank.

Linneville, Kirkfieldbank.

The bridge at Kirkfieldbank was originally built in 1699. A new bridge was built in 1959.

The two bridges today.

Kirkfieldbank looking down from the Lanark Brae.

War memorial, Kirkfieldbank.

108

This photograph shows Kirkfieldbank village and was given to me by Ronnie Porteous whose grandmother owned the Kirkfieldbank Hotel and Greenrig farm.

The caravan site is still very popular today and is not dissimilar to this scene of yesteryear. *Courtesy of Bill Moir.*

The Clyde Valley Hotel, Kirkfieldbank. *Courtesy of the Hamilton Advertiser.*

Mousehill, near Lanark. The Mouse River runs nearby. Mousemill was built in 1795 and the local residents were obliged to buy flour from there.

Cartland Bridge, near Lanark. The bridge was built in 1822 by John Gibb, of Aberdeen, from a design by Thomas Telford.

The Cartland Bridge Hotel was opened in 1962 and was converted from this spectacular mansion house. *Courtesy of the Hamilton Advertiser*.

The dining room of the Cartland Bridge Hotel.
Courtesy of the Hamilton Advertiser.

The monument to Major General William Roy,
responsible for the Ordnance Survey.

HERE STOOD
MILTONHEAD
THE BIRTHPLACE OF
MAJOR-GENERAL
WILLIAM ROY
4TH MAY 1726 — 30TH JUNE 1790
FROM WHOSE MILITARY MAP OF
SCOTLAND MADE IN 1747-1755
GREW THE ORDNANCE SURVEY
OF GREAT BRITAIN

The memorial plaque on the monument.

Hallbar Tower is a mediaeval tower house and was once known as Braidwood Tower.

Corehouse stands a short distance from Corra Castle and was restored in 1983. It is open to the public during August and is owned by Lt Col. and Mrs Cranstoun.

Corra Linn, one of the Falls of Clyde. William and Dorothy Wordsworth were just two of the many notable people to visit the falls and Wordsworth wrote *In Corra's Glen* to commemorate his visit.

Bonnington Linn, another of the spectacular falls in the gorge.

It is easy to see how Wordsworth was inspired when you look at this view of Bonnington Falls.

Bonnington Power Station harnesses some of the energy from the river.

Bonnington Mains farm.

Bonnington Linn once more.

Previous and present page: More views of the spectacular waterfalls. You can take a walk down the gorge past all of this. The view and the noise are really something.

BONNINGTON, FALLS OF CLYDE, LANARK.

Ten
A Last Look at Lanark

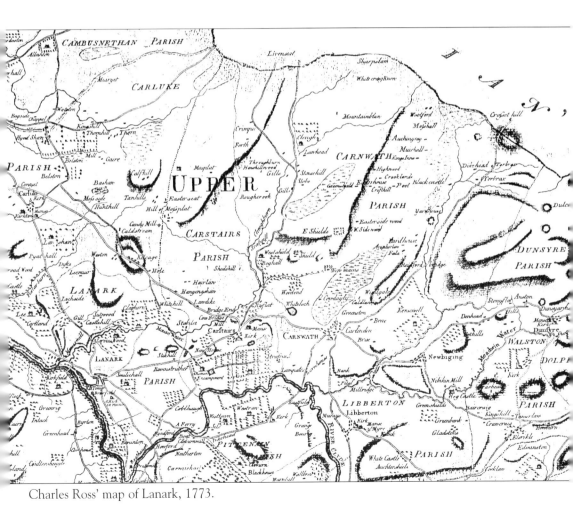

Charles Ross' map of Lanark, 1773.

The statue of Wallace on the old St Nicholas church.

122

On the left of this view of Castlegate is the monument which shows where Sir William Wallace's house stood.

The graveyard at St Kentigern's church in Hyndford Road. In the background is the crypt of Wiliam Smellie, the obstetrician.

The plaque on the crypt of William Smellie in St Kentigern's churchyard. The plaque was erected in 1931.

Lanark sewage works. Not exactly the kind of 'wish you were here' view! *Courtesy of Hamilton Advertiser*.

St Mary's Roman Catholic cemetery.

The burial place of a covenanter.

The old toll house at Hyndford Bridge. The bridge was built in 1773.

Looking over the loch to the Lanark Loch Hotel.

The High Street looking down towards St Nicholas church. *Courtesy of Hamilton Advertiser.*

The Vogue cinema viewed from the station. The Vogue is, like many cinemas, now a Bingo hall.

Bloomgate.

The North Vennel.